If I Should Say I Have Hope

IF I
SHOULD
POEMS LYNN MELNICK
SAY I
HAVE
HOPE

For Jayleen :) J.

YesYes Books ➳ Blacksburg, VA

for Timothy Donnelly
everything and always

CONTENTS

ONE

Sacré Cœur

In my worries I am plummeting down steps,
industrial, medieval, breezy welcome

stairs like little landings where a foot could catch.
In some nightmares my breasts are so misshapen

they are no longer mammalian, quite,
this inevitable evolution we can't call progress.

Those mornings I wake exactly as I fell,
a little upright, on my back, static and sweaty

and always next to you. Call it relief
to find everything as it was, though one summer I fell up

and up and up and it was a good lesson
in the sham of gravity.

And once, when we found ourselves in another summer
overlooking an entire city, we thought

we couldn't get older or higher,
though in my worries I am both, and falling.

These Pretty Years

All night I am ugly, wryneck whore, fantastic misshape.
I cannot stop eating or the eyes, shut and measured
in gloating. Walked convulsive to a bedroom you know

better, demanded proper attentions. What in a waist
is to be proud of? When I was fat you were fine
and now I am indistinct: systolic hysteric, weak

even to the corner to the train, sure I will be stalled
and gassed, that there should be value in a death.
What has passed came trying to rise from cement,

might have carried us steamy both with sturdier legs.
I will lie down with you; I will get up with you.
And then: just a day again, small scratches from the testing

of knives to my flesh, the endless face-scrubbing
with will not to waste these pretty years. Something
like folly has infected my blood. I imagine my life

would change with a girl's given name, heading off
somewhere on a street of strangers put to bump
and suffocate. I cannot realize the evolution of this act.

I must have walked because I am still walking.

Forecast

Hauled uphill by lightning's premonition
I follow what soil

one flower cropped from,
the calla lily that bloomed lonely from the compost,

a garland for our finish.
Oh, electricity. It's never quite enough.

When we need an iridescent witness
it only sputters, atingle

from a thundercloud and bent on destruction.
Happy New Year. I loved you

because you dared not love me back,
sexy or drowsy or vanishing,

each hour before midnight
the lusty mirror to all that's angry after.

Maybe I'm dead for the vultures
freeing themselves from last night's feast

of dread and diddling, knocking them
back at the farewell party. At the welcome buffet

I let you pull my hair,
throw me to the rocks,

I write because just to make sense of meaning to understand and to forget what I understand. compleatly fun, to forget.

I write to make messes to find beauty when I am ugly, ugly like a furless cat bitter about the cuteness lost in the drain from the owner that washed it off.

11

disarrange me.
It's your knack for filth

that keeps me begging for beauty in the rotting soil.
Tell me how I grew from garbage,

tell me how lethal, how lovely I am.

Weird Winter

They are wrong: one can die from heat
or one can die weeded and bland. Shoes
will forget they walked ever down steps
so long down grounded. Perhaps you wait

for flowers. Six years is not much
to be gone as you return each night
to witness this piercing mess, scattered
and salty. I am going to finish what

I started while you are a ghost to prick
me less. The brown tones of near sleep
states bring days to this body with rumble;
little to love is wet or looking to be

washed in pastel. You would and will,
by which I mean, go away. Saying: out,
saying there was that day once I remember
a walk through Hollywood with blue face

and drugged to the church where they
told me surely I could not be a nun.
Even if I wanted empty in my gut, not food
or dream or man. I would be girl born

in weird winter of a different faith,
halter top and wretched and going to live
years after and years after I take
your shoes off at the door, ask you

weightless to move in, choose any corner
you need. Watch me eat meals and meals,
watch me unwashed and ugly. See this life
linger like affliction and daybreak.

There Was a Child Who Never Wanted

I'm laughing at her, that red-cheeked doll, my storm-of-the-century.
    She is icicles!

I'm hoarding odd gallons, dreaming of fear.
    There was a child who never wanted

and she was redolent and wild, taintless light
    and heinous yes, she was beautiful, mild.

And here's yours truly, speaking of love, again.
    How ordinary. I'm afraid I'm untrussed and strutted:

hold me. And don't be ridiculous.

There's some kind of crazy on the way, a frill of brown,
    storm clouds or smoke. Cities fall like this

though you think you hold them
    in your head in the distance behind you.

Though you think you notice disaster, you do not.
    Oh she is precious

one foot in the dirt. A red and spreading
    smudge at her knees, white leg whitest

for she never wants sun pinning into her
      tender, razing perfection. My love leaves me

overcharged and spoiled for others; my love
      leaves me bored in stranger company, *fuck*

fucking like a trash-mouth. One minute I'm sitting on the sink
      lacking red shoes

and chewing myself, the next I've grown
      into my heels begging for more. Her mouth

corners me slyly, arms straight as her
      unformed sides. I want to be that frigid. I want

nothing expected of me and my morning.

Sorrow, with Some Eye Contact

Mostly you just disappear. When I don't see you dead
I know you're alive. I can see you by the clothes you're wearing,

by your boot print on the unloved grass.
We make an ugly street ugly, a giant room stripped,

its high wood beams and bed big enough for six of me
or three of us. You swear we have no roof.

One morning we counted chickens
and ate their eggs for breakfast. We played with hats.

I think I thought your weight was on me
but you were vanishing, even as you sculpted us from clay.

Someone has shown up for me, I sense a chariot,
the sky preparing to rain on everything.

We forgot to put the doves away.
I can barely see you. I think someone has shown up for me,

can you see headlights? Hear footsteps?
Some remember my snatching an outstretched hand.

And in a room of rafters you do what must be done
under moonlight, though it's days before you are found,

chickens gone, doves in trees, my bust smashed and mouth
punched in so its grin runs into an eye, winking.

Choking You

I am strings from my garment, suddenly loud,
a sight with more skin than hands. I went to each home
with you for a very long time. Up in a bungalow
with ankles and tender, you sleep from substance

so goodnight sweetheart. Let me glance at your neck,
pasty and frail. Let me think how easy it would be.
Forget the guesthouse where you struck me to the floor
in spinning beverage: inevitable. I am still a gypsy,

a bloodsport, a worm. One hundred essays on the same subject.
But look my beloved at the quilt I made; I didn't
lift a finger. Shall I address, undress, haul you back
from air? Are you perhaps yet dead? You and me,

we're sticky and frantic, we're tired but I, being more
grown with my own roof above, can sleep now too,
knowing if I left, taking my hands with me, yours
would still be there, unsure, unstrung, and choking you.

The Uselessness of Legs in the First Place

I.
My heels in their terry socks

digging into the beige
Southern California carpet frantic
like sand crabs
but getting nowhere

or more like foolish tires
in a far-off snow bank

burying me deeper into trouble.

2.
Here are some things that my legs once were
but then never were:

fetal, chubby, less chubby,
strong, restless, covered in ballet pink,

uncovered, crossed, uncrossed

covered in denim,
covered in a kind of homemade hoop skirt,

covered in the last instance of the emptying of a coin purse

before everything about myself changed
and suddenly I'm sensing the uselessness of legs in the first place.

3.
Pinned underneath a person

to hell with tires to hell with far-off snow banks to hell with

when the sand of Southern California
played carpet to this outrage hands down,
legs up, lungs crashing.

Done for.

Lagoon

When I was fifteen, tight and brash in love, I read
the Brontës and the weeklies each night after work
and before you, whose thirst and ribs astounded.

You would be reading something by Bukowski,
something about a woman who maybe fucked
rosebuds and flinched. You brought me a flower

from a package weak with flowers from the fill-station
food mart, but I would not let you put it inside me,
what with my head of voices and dazzled housecalls,

what with the smell of hot dogs and gas all over that rose.
But that isn't possible. No. But is this?
I had chosen you, in brown rooms, in laundries,

chosen you self-sown, best, but do not think of you
often. Still I find myself here, and the voices find me
again recounting splinters. *Is this what you did?*

Yes. I waded in head-smut and sand. You brought me,
bit and dreary, into what you named lagoon
(but was mostly rainwater). Yes I knew better then;

yes I didn't. *Is this what you did?* Meaning: *You did this.*

Dance You Monster to My Soft Song!

I'm walking twice-pace home as these days will be darker
    and might we be enlightened, maybe.

Hueish and fancy. This is how I have always
    drawn myself. Skirted, level, not half

so spiral as what, as me. This is how I have always
    and suffer it

sordid in the glass, downcast
    and teeming. I have seen myself

with tambourine and candelabra, folded down
    with cymbal, turned

dancing from exclamation, but what am I really but lazy, lacy, looped.

Ouija-struck once in this ghost
    weather I cried that fool's cry, gutted:

They're waiting for me, love, in new rooms to terrify.

Altering darkly and by centimeter.
    What is this ogre, hovering in mad air? A bloom, a pick,

a specimen jarred so decorously
    carnival I watch it ugly with its lips and hooks and eyes, my monster

abusing as the harmonium. I hate
    the tinker and the droning on of it.

I must slump presently to bed, coat
    kicked toward the window of wind-

blown chatter, in a twist of down
    and wool: all saints point toward you

though I am hollowed from what
    I swallowed years ago, forced under

in a California pool. I might rise to change the radio
    but I almost never made it to you. I must rise

to change the radio, repeating.

Shade

You could come back soon, unpacked
knife to threaten, rough-grabbed
pout and piquant blade. I am always
squared to fear, turning in quick

rhythms in sick sun to find myself
safe with no bad hand in mine and ever
returning home. How easy to harrow
in that room where you kept me and I

kept myself sot. Things exquisite
should be sought out. I loved you not
aging, I loved you devout and you did
not disappoint. Elegy for you is your

never leaving. Careful, I find you
tucked away knickknack and remnant.
The word for me is drastic and the word
for you is ghost. And what has name

I love still: this is what want has done.

TWO

The Rain Is Over, Apparently

Wild west of here, where snow
is more often rain

and more often still the bluest skies
you'd never seen,

there are paid professionals
monitoring the climate situation.

We don't change, but there's proof
that some things do, the clouds

a pleasant bloat
all these states later, like we haven't known

for days, not since we last
licked each other's wounds,

drowning out the violence
with violence, making our own

scars with bits of broken anything
closer and closer

to the heart, beating
whatever's beating us

to the punch, no matter
the hour, whatever the weather.

Yom Kippur

On holiest day dismal I digest myself, composed.
There will be one of these each year, specific apology,

each sin. That of horrible tongue, cut-rusted, that
of proud wash-out. And what mad break this fast

on an untoward day, head spinning. I saw a man
once die. Touched his vacant body, wet his stomach

until my eyes turned at his passing in self-scented
clothes. Now I bind in white, wed to what is done

is wrong. Such terrible dragging of lipstick across
a smart mouth to divide it. Such greed. Such intention.

Lucky

This is no place for autumn
and the pumpkins wonder how they got to this patch
in this lot, in this city.

They're wincing at the weather, looking up my skirt,
making orange a kind of festive
and not like the sun at all

until we go home. If at home there's a man named Lucky
then at home there's a man named Lucky.
That's his rattletrap, that's his knife a baton in his fingers.

I can feel blood running down my arms.
It's ninety-seven degrees.
The putrid seeded center pours like bile onto newspaper.

Breezes float through the only known window.
This house wasn't meant to be a house.
There are three rooms and none of them a kitchen.

We don't know where to keep the knives.
A long, long time ago I was gleaming with what I wanted
to be. And I'll tell you what.

One afternoon, I fucked a man in three different rooms
because I didn't know how to leave.
Sometimes I took rides home from strangers,

sometimes I was those strangers.
I was a hot spell in a dry heat.
Nothing should take as long as time is taking me.

Amusing or Diverting, Not Such Fun

Last night I did it. Pulled strands, tripled round my wrist
    until snapped. I'll wreck it if it's good. Last night

the gate rattled before the window boxed with mums,
    some almost purple and shouldn't last much past.

I'll wake to my watching their devastation in the rain.
    Things are moving along without me, my blood

drawn melting into tubes, a twisted heat and moan
    roting words crookedly to trance me. I'm wrong

in this room, utensil-wrung stubborn and steel.
    I don't want a body, not with what's inside.

Look at me: I will be young once and waste it
    on fluster, ounce for ounce unpounded weight

and pounded flesh. Cake and fig forced frantic
    in the mouth, beef and cream cracker forced out

through the same. I do this with willpower. A miracle—
    even come winter. Last night, my one room

betrayed me, forced me dizzy to look in the glass.
    Small dress coiling each brutish hip. It was grim,

the turn of events that turned into this. A room
    full of specialists, an air machine, a mystery aspirin.

Who but who didn't want me charming?
　　Attentive! Eyelash, desire; tobacco and fabric.

Please, there's a cocktail napkin woefully bare.
　　Here's what they said when I painted my face:

You should always. But I fear each stairwell, flights
　　and iron flights to ascend to and if I am starlet

I am starlet on the landing, overlooking sea-level,
　　eclipsing occasion. It is occasion why we're here.

I'm new today and shaking with it. They're looking
　　at me looking at me. Splendid! A fainting! I am best

when I dabble in consciousness and a soundly
　　spinning room. This calls for cake to sugar its spell

on a hard, selfish crowd: Oh look little one you have grown
　　to older. Oh lovely one you will turn still colder.

Monstrous

I should have left when you left and not be
     exhausted in a walk-up, years past, wasted fantastic

and underdressed, strenuously cold, cold

and blinding. Steam heat tricks its hissing out to grease
     the walls and stick me molded to the sheets.

     I must think of you always
          to know you are not here.

Drawn of it bloody, bitten myself porcelain
     and fainted for this mess of shade and floorboard.

And now the smell of maggot, crisp and feeding

curbside on rot and poundcake. Steady feast
     as you are mine, smog on this numbered street,

this afterlife reason I cannot see between.

     My God, I am imperfect—
          a heart at my throat

wishing for a wooded, a slope, a junction, whatever

not knowing where to step, mound of hybrid

branches or dunghill mushroom, whatever silly
   from the impact. Bound to you by air and fleshless

and what could almost—*Listen, 'tis just the hour,*

the awful time—save me. There are so many ways
   for a body to yield monstrous

but I do not know how to die
   to be where I would not see you:

         just glass between us, just universe.

One

One year I was rich, clasped
rigid in red, hair tedious all night
to music woozy and wicked,

glasses off squinting to watch one depart
then another. Witnessed veins
give out under needle or saw them

else trying to come back
on a hospital table, thumb
buttoning to sleep-death

and death itself. One year I was gone
when a shotgun blasted one
mean temple, mastered the arch

of back for sadness, the run through
plotted scrub. Now I am gauged
in climax clutter of scrap

photograph, waiting for the next
to go. I am good at grief, know
the twist of one deliberate dead

that can ensanguine a heart. I spell eternity
over and over as lullaby. I wait
plundered, the last to live, several.

Of Being Lost Forever

You've been careless over all, her dress left thrashing
with the others in a heap and jostle. You've been finding its beads

in odd places: the shower drain, between fork prongs.
These beads that she put one by one on the two-tone sea foam

years ago. In the weeks after you knew she was dead,
when they had buried her in another dress, you traveled

to a house not your own and knew a darkness then, a long
winding walk around what you had always called a corner,

a snuck darkness so sudden that there was a pleasing thought
of being lost forever. The summer before you knew

she was dying there were nights you couldn't sleep
for the pounding. If you were branded femme-fatale

there'd be a gun on your nightstand, but here
there is only air too still to rustle. There'd be a man under-bed

saying *Sure, your heart should hammer and should never stop*
and just when you're naked and dozing on the sheet,

that's when the phone rings. The air is sticking. Foolish girl,
you think you will be a sweeping force and the world

will be kind. Tune in tomorrow for the gruesome conclusion. You should see it now because I see it now. Pick it up.

You wouldn't know happy if it kissed you on the mouth.

And If Thou Wilt, Forget

All are ghost faces, and all of us sick
walking in our own sick skin. I am myself
here to avoid you, hovering always
in what sour room I have called home

and stuck to, tempered. Gusty you,
in and out of brick-backed windowpane
watching as I lift from water each steamed
appendage to cleanse, lips cracking

with the mirror to snap my head against.
On the street I am one manic holler
of a shuttered mouth, pallid and terrified
of gesture. What of fullness? Weed-eyed,

I purchase bread to prolong this unslept
body. What of return? Not for another night
swept shut in the plaster of place. Darling,
love is not always found in the same ways.

Spirited, I would be gladly slept and slept
more. Not to join you in your drunken jaunts
of haunting. I would be dead, my dead one,
and should not return to find me.

Casino

Here it's so hot we burn without sunlight:
    a misstep on the pavement, purple-faced and heaving.

Here is winning up ahead, extra-everlasting
    what winning there is! Here water spouts dazzle

fixed to music overwhelming, and it overwhelms.
    Here most flesh is overflesh, mammoth or rawhide

crawling aswarm. Example: "Do you think
    that girl will dance with me?" Answer: "Go for broke!"

So follow an aspect to the bottom with silver,
    say we are lesser. In legend we are lesser. Here

there is no fervor anymore if ever there was, only
    wholly dazed craving. We are catastrophe, let's say it

together. Here we cannot leave more fairly beyond neon.
    We could run for the roof beams unhinged with prospect.

We could devote our entirety to the glamorous void.
    Example: "To be successful is to decide exactly

what you want. Go, then, for broke." We sink to the center
    with cups, slots, quarters. Vampiric, conquered.

If the center opens, an arrow runs through with a maze
    back to center. What dread in our slaughtered selves,

this brilliant illness years on end. Here twenty-three
of each one hundred thousand take their lives.

This is expected after an evening, though we surprise
ourselves showing in the clanging smoke. What dream

we had, what they said was such. A push from the bed
toward the night-crawlers stiff with indoor element,

wildest lark. Example: "Sure as you are sure, are you sure
you want all your money on a pony?" Answer:

"Yes. I am broken!" We walk the most astonishing carpet
now each time underground, where the cooler species

gather, the sorts seize to all look sad. We remain only
more towards dawn in gross proximity of skins

that whirl around the masts. Here we are adapting, greenhouse,
a jingling theater of torso or we don't know who we are,

want less of what we don't know but go on stunned.
Anger replaces fear replaces hunger, being so twinkly

grand. Yards of Technicolor beverage, decaying spread
of backside slapped to a barstool when the glass and the

gloss and the barstool tumble and we've jumped, boy, we've
jumped, our very stake listen what plunged our heart.

Blackout

What's left open but booze and pin-up,
a generator humming that called your car to park.

We're finished with beauty:
inner beauty, sloppy beauty, my beauty.

Once upon a time you fashioned a collapse
and called it us, what we would have called living

had there been less cocaine.
Is rage what felled the power line, what strapped us to these seats?

Truth is, you did love me more.
We're close enough to home to die here

and I have known you too long
to wither flashlit in the passenger seat.

How long will you plead me brute and fearless
when each time I stop just before dawn.

Diorama

1.
I wanted to see the rats,

the local rats and the exotic rats,
strung up and stretched out

and taxidermied behind display glass,
this before I realized I would find taxidermy

a kind of refreshing hobby in an age before we could all just
find each other again.

> *And what do you think is in there, under all that shine?*
>
> *A frosting can, a big one; a tombstone,*
> *but like the falling apart kind, like what would be*
> *in the old country or the wild west;*
> *a soda can, a big one; a drain plug for the ocean;*
> *a robot, oh I don't know, isn't that enough answers?*

2.
Something here smacks of that seaside hotel
which was hardly by the sea

and hardly a hotel somewhere southwest of Yosemite
in that part of California no one believes you about.

But it's in front of us, behind glass under lights,
blue blue electric blue

and what some would say is cowhide,
so it must have been

good, been real, and been by the sea.
Here it is.

Oh, there it is. It gets prettier. It's beautiful.

Lake Tahoe: California Side, Nevada Side

Driving east where snow would fall
I am trying to keep us
awake. Skunks are spraying mercilessly.
A mountain lion killed a hometown girl not thirty
miles from here. I was meant for somebody else.

There are bad flags at all the truck stops.
Right now, midwinter, a midwinter's sun on my face;
right now, history notwithstanding, butch passersby
notwithstanding; right now, I will be naked in a hotel
with wood-paneled walls, a buck head at check-in.

The silk of my sweater is cruel, we're gasping for air.
If you had suggested that I had been kidnapped,
that I was here against what will I have left,
that it isn't really me you're fucking,
the sheets not stained with either of us,

that we win every penny back we thought vanished
in a distressing thick of smoke;
if you had told me that you know I hate
hiking, all-you-can-eat, the smell of silk,
I would not have entered the teepee we stumbled upon

littered with our kind of wrapper,
I would not have entered this would-be adventure
already spent, my hands gripping guidebooks
to other cities, where animals are leashed or caged,
where you could not find or follow.

Mojave

I.

Los Angeles stays warm through winter. You know this. You know
this desert where we come to, this foul outhouse

that binds with wood and those who eat. Here, unless there are lights
there is no light. I cannot drive as you did, but I can wipe

your mouth, cover your punctured arm with your sleeve. I will not watch you
die on the carpet. It would be as if I had never been here.

2.

We are guests at an hour told to go home; sun and bells ring
in humble interval. We are what breaks in season, a homely

outgrowth, boring. I cause you no heartache with my indifference,
even your limbs bend toward mine. My nose hurts in desert air,

in bars where I am unwelcome even as I pretend to be famous
for seduction. Sleep is what does not come when as much as I want it.

3.

You pick up every glowing penny, let them burn your hands
unrecognizable until you find yourself holding out your luck

all the way up route ten. You consider then how your father
once told you that you had a skinny neck, how you held onto that,

logged it as a sign of heart. It could happen; this man could
pull you to the back seat. And what if he took your straw hair

into his crusted hands and yanked so hard as to break your neck.
Possible. Almost becoming. So when you arrive at another

unbroken wild, dust left dust under feet, you will say to yourself:
What haven't I known? Who haven't I loved all my life?

THREE

When California Arrives It Lasts All Year

Dreadful sorry and packed for balmy air,
I've no use for this shudder of adventure,
these conspiracy-worn streets puffed with pollen and froth.

There's nothing like nurture to seduce a frontier
into collapse. In a cavern, in a canyon,
violet roses hung like bats.

I bend myself over the bed this time
just to see if I break, and when I don't
I belly up, sick from the rotten bill of goods

I keep selling myself, herring boxes without tops.
It's not that I didn't exist here,
ankle deep in the foaming brine.

I have tried to keep the chalkboard clean
even as dust clapped a cloud about my head. I came here to learn, no?
And all I do is cover my ears. Please, no more recollection.

I can't hear you. I can't hear you.

Everybody In!

It's not much of a lie to say I hate the outdoors.
Something about discomfort.

But it's a lie when I say that I don't, spitting
on my arm to rub off the layers, what failed to wash.

Sometimes it works and sometimes it doesn't
but if I were asked again I'd say let's skip

the hot drive down, the mockingbird, the digging,
cold coffee with radical strangers, fellow Americans,

wrong-headed love, dunes, rocks, retro round eyewear,
nudity, big ideas, destitute children,

overwhelming stucco suburbs, dubious rafts,
cold waiting, makeshift dinners, communal bathrooms,

piles of quarters, and all the lying.
I spent one hundred dollars on a camera that would document this.

Is there a California I don't know about?
Smaller, I finished a day floating after everyone left the pool.

There was barking and laughter. I can't tread water
but I can master flotation to save myself.

Tanked

Turning first splendid then empty of feature
Mirror makes lover a thousand gutted husks

This is how water maddens us how crowds
Compel our dismal faces against glass

Neither hook nor shake of saddest human finger
Tail and tail in merciless direction

That's Not Funny; You Clowns Don't Make Me Laugh

The woman in the grocery store on Sunset
stopped me in the produce,

her claws about my shoulders,
to warn me that I might be an angel,

to bless me on behalf of her God,
on behalf of the lady who bleached her hair

past the point hair can withstand
so each strand became a defiance of her very God

and her outsize lips could only up and down
until what we think of as prophecy

was merely opening wide to say ah.
I took my remains and broke free,

my skin loose as I ran. Meanwhile
the butcher I'm dancing with refuses to change my face.

And the dye that spilled on the floor?
The kind of red your mother warned you about.

But no one warned me, I drank it straight.
Or hadn't you heard. Lately, it seems,

plastic surgeons are murdered far more frequently
than your more interior doctors.

How have I missed that crazy little thing
called conversion, when I could have called it that?

The plastic surgeons scalpel their tombstones;
it's not that they wanted to die,

they only wished to right the wrong bodies.
Was the cause perfection? Whose isn't. But everyone's face

is falling, and I don't want the circus come to town,
whether I'm the circus or the town.

Yom Kippur

The capital building is on fire again,
flames distress the air at twenty stories.

We've all read the demolition logs, how twenty-nine follows thirty
and you see how I'm counting down,

in order, though the elements skipped and hopped to it,
ruining men, which is what elements do.

Is that God there, burning the house down?

My finger, tipped red, traces sins by the dozen.
I am a secret that anyone

with X-ray vision and a taste for flesh could expose.
I'm so humble I could kick your ass.

Ah, hello, sin of the smart mouth.

Slap, bellow, slap, showboat.
And hello sin of unloving, of taking it all back.

This autumn, the bees disprove the dire science.
They lurch toward the only syrup they know

and we give sweet up, afraid to eat; we wind up here,
this group confession, this smother of bodies, cotton and canvas.

This is what I'm talking about.
The grassland encircling town smolders, a rope of incineration.

We skip-hop and skip-hop over it.
We're on our toes, we're on our heels,

we're on our heels, are we on our knees? Get on your knees,
this ain't no good girl's holiday.

A Genie Serves a Continental Breakfast, Angel Brings the Desired

She casts one spell slammed to the bedcovers
sweating, anguished, lovesick. But you want

her to remain intact (intact and on two feet)
to deliver herself in a tablet, herself in an ashtray

and beg for your most appealing heart in spring.
She has knotted a scarf of wings for you, outlined

your commandments: champagne in a certain glass,
foolishly again. Some lovesome music sets her

sorry, though she cries for herself, in your hall
of flutter in a fine fantastic get-up, hinged to the plain

sad bells. Is this meant to bend her murky
then so be murky. A second from nothingness, its flutter,

spin, tear. Every day a different coat, an odder step
and shiver. (Ask a stupid girl a stupid question.)

God made of someone an error and it's up in lights,
each to astonish by pink, white, finally dramatic.

All aglow, all winter long. (A stupid answer here.)

A Description Is Not a Birthday

The gong I ring
rings riddled with helium
and exhaustion, swings me

heavenward to prick
a cloud turned to glue.
It's true, the desert that housed me

bewitched my eyes for anything
past their own tint.
Where I come from

people seek to levitate
but I could not cross my own body;
put me in an empty room

and it's an empty room.
And when I finally rose
I hit the glass so hard

blood striped my face
and I swallowed it hard
just to stay alive.

Seven Scenes from the Wreckage

I.

In a sallow square, five by five faces project a mood
    toward a sharp-nosed dog with felt ears.

We're a mess of lapel, wallpaper, denim
    and I'm in a dress of apples.

That boy above me in the checkered jacket,
    he'll grow up to kiss me on a porch

then pollute me in a pool house—a tacky
    set piece, as these things go. I counted the turquoise

tile edging the water, and when I lost tally

I began again, my face pressed cruelly
    into wicker, my eyes peering through

the breaks in its twist.

And then a gift, when I still believed in all that.

    It rained in August, droplets
        snapping from the overlay

like blown glass breaking blue, magnificent.

2.

There was sand in my hourglass and gold on the beach
    blown through the spray,

through the shiny suit among a grove
    of options.

Sometimes a hand would unfold on nuggets of foil
    from a box of cigars.

This when I was very small
    and through to another state's recreational triumph

where I dug greedily for prizes. It's not visible
    for the grainy murk clung to the lens, for the hair

whipping my face, but I was smiling.

I was dozens of girls back then, and some of them happy.
    Miles after, there is the Rogue River

recklessly collecting tributaries, the seagulls
    splitting their time between residences.

The water there is furious enough for daredevils
    but I had no use for it.

3.
Suddenly I liked avocados, California's own plan
    to fatten me up, to ripen itself

    under my grip before rotting the fruit
        as a metaphor for time.

I was rotations away from an ability to fathom.

That was the year my instamatic broke,
    the end to fuzzy four-sides of goings-on,

of me topless in so many stairwells I'd bore
    even my biographer, wheezing at the top step.

Months left me where I couldn't laugh.

I knew a kid with a balcony edging his bedroom

overlooking the busiest intersection
    I'd spent instances overlooking. He had to jump

and I took home that obstinate plant
    urged from a wide-mouthed jar.

4.

Around an L-shaped table she couldn't suppose
    that I'm an L, formal in a month

of pedestrian secrets, dumb to the pretty teeth
    whittling themselves to fangs.

She anchored the pileup of people I wore out,
    persuading from one trouble to

the next

to demonstrate a kind of shade, even as nineteen eighty-nine
    was my warmest year on record.

Like a rat sated on slop, my place on the food chain
    had yet to be

decided.

And in all the goodbyes, I only caught her
    sideways, where she fancied me

well enough to tell me what I'd become. Too remote,
    that kind of chaos, when I'd already

given up.

5.
Someone lost an elbow out the window of a bus,
    clipped by a six ton truck.

How does the body reset itself
    when the time for downy regeneration has long since

sunk into relentless decay?

It doesn't, of course, but I think the lesson
    is to keep trying, and to keep

your limbs to yourself.

Days later, a man with nine fingers
    charmed me over a fence to listen

to the loons exulting a lake in the winter range
    because there is no winter here.

I shot a self portrait and it caught my white belly
    and behind it

the red light of leaving.

Now we must also leave me, tramping
    in a modern radiation, blooming home.

6.
I took anyone who'd come with me to pose
    at the orange-lit rows

of dire wolf heads, maybe hundreds of them
    gone skeletal

as even the ruthless will.
    The flash never got it,

turned the background yellow
    as if in a bright kitchen

a pack sat down to a meal
    and stayed on for centuries.

We've all had that happen.

The redundancy of death
    left me rapt against the scratch

of the back wall. I thought a lot about tar
    not realizing the pits I stuck in

were a mire of effervescent
    obsession. I wrongly predicted

what feasted on me would be less easily
    pleased, less patient as I sank.

7.
Should I have been terrified
   when flat surfaces

became uphill, reddening
   my cheeks? They called it

infection but I knew it was
   allergy, a reaction to

all the gravel and under-
   brush and moss. I was

desperate for pavement,
   something solid to crack

me open, something porous
   to absorb the stain.

I would have been any person
   who would house me.

In one image I'm in brown
   hiking boots, fumbling

with matches in the thicket.
   Afterwards, I bought shoes

nothing could accommodate,
   patent lime green with

extra-large buckles and a trick
   to the heel. These I

photographed from above,
   with the toes pointed

westward, because I thought
   I would never escape.

FOUR

Manhattan Valley

But who am I if not outside, a blizzard and borrowed
but hardly noticed, a drizzle? Let's look at this objectively.

I am always cold. Every step is street water, spell
surrounds the building. It must be noticed, to wail out

sirens grandly, to scarlet a sky this stern and dreary.
Lightning has let me live one more storm.

It's embarrassing, for God's sake, how I stay.
Here in our hollow, the bulbs grow impossibly up,

waiting for a comeback. Tell me what this downcast
means and I will tell you where I've run from, a street

with strains of summer, a room that cannot hold us
in its grave drapery. I know you so well here; I keep

always in the same arrangement, lolling extravagant,
sinful, buried in possession. This is lucky and lucky

isn't what it used to be, for either of us. Most times
I am too unbraced to bear it, quite soprano and flung.

Where is the hand at my waist, the dancing?
Not some tricked-out voodoo, but what's all around me.

I miss you, you can't even imagine. Sometimes I bite
to bleeding: I need on a grander scale. Only, everywhere

there are rules, which means it can't be this cozy forever.
Hat on the bed, shoes on the table. We are doomed.

Sane

They kept me there youngest
　　on a small bed, eating lobster

from pliant trays as if born
　　that way, put solitary often

for touching inside gowns.
　　Bless my heart for I would

have one, repulsive and quick.
　　I was beautiful for three months,

learned the nervy stench
　　of a clean body. Wanted one

long sentence, one patch
　　of white wall, wished, resolutely,

to drop to my knees. I loved
　　myself. Years after, I wore

hospital lotion like an antique
　　shoe, blue-daisy-bottled and kind.

I grew wily, knew sane people,
　　practiced dying with vitamins.

If I Should Say I Have Hope

It was chance not to have kept
a closed body. I was taught
how to writhe, did allow each
man to strike me ten times with

my own fist. Autumn comes
stumped and nauseous. You
will not be home, woke there
gull-eaten and put. This is how

it had been for us: to say *where
you go, I will go.* I scratched
your street into my arm and there
was only blood and no way

to find you. The ticking of clocks
will not keep me calm. Notice
these great arms, stretched
up to the water-stained ceiling.

Imagine these hands, fractured
again and fixed as new. Tomorrow
I believe I will eat breakfast.
Terse morning, I will want to.

In Which Our Heroine's Past Is Recounted and Future Foretold

Well hello, you—animated, angry, motionless
    but for your mouth, which purses

and opens, simulating what a mouth does. Once again

you have lost yourself ahead of a large glass.
    Your torment stays dead, a suicide,

and you have reinvented your hips
    and what they do in water, on land, on impact,

at this boulevard bar, the wide lanes of traffic
    between you and a bus depot, and so anywhere.

Where am I? you think. But aren't you always
    in love? If by strange turn you mean

how you erased him completely then things
    took a strange turn, took on a gloom to replace

all the intoxicating fun you hadn't

been having. You think, *We tried not wanting
    to break any heart, not wanting to be*

extraordinary. You think, *Matter has hit my body
    but the pitching arm is buried.*

And yet the great *Over* of this great experiment
    goes on rising from the tides, mutated

and reeking. Look forward, chickadee—
    In at least three countries you can name, you will be in love.

You will visit five formidable churches, kneeling

down in a modest skirt to fondle inlaid stone;
    the droplets sprung from the sinking of a coin

will splash your chest just enough to remind you
    you're getting warm. When he goes on

without you, it's a lonely few minutes, but he always
    comes right back.

When he is done, you are done, and you, he.
    So bottoms up, chickadee, you should really

get out more. Somewhere in this town
    your torment's bones rattle and spin, sequence a chain

that's yours if you want it. Once again
    you have lost yourself behind a panic of fingers.

Your fingers smell like saltwater. You've had a crush
    on saltwater since before your torment

slapped your faultless mouth. You shouldn't get out more,

your mouth is sullied, a threat to itself, hooked
    on the inhale, a pain upon breathing.

Somewhere in this town, your torment's bones

await you, gorgeous from a distance, afraid to stop
    talking, better than you remember.

Coney Island

I give the red-topped toy machine back its decal
as I want something else, better, what you have:

rubber replica of reptile, shock-purple and sinister.
The small business of setting out to do a day

that started evening last with soup and summer
boredom ended here, asleep once more, clutch

of fear in the sand. Concession calls to wake us
and we are two among the hunched, invisible

to the well-oiled grotesque. For retribution,
a four-ticket ride, eyes spun from upside-down.

I bite and cannot scream. Next whiskey
at a boardwalk bar, a watered-down one of my own.

I could now dance like this pair by the jukebox:
resolved, fat and furrowed. But I am not ugly

yet or cheered. I want a room to keep a home.
I want a bed. (Lemonade. Sand again. Subway.)

Let me sleep on your lap. No tracks to cross
bridges; we are going underwater. Whatever we have done

has sun-marked a line flat to my flesh. It hurts
like want hurts: that sweet. The rare side of no.

Town & Country

When my friends were dying
    back in the city, I was pretty damn healthy

out in the country, sitting on the taut taupe leather
    of the passenger side, always the passenger side.

I liked to look out the cold car window

hoping the sun wouldn't rise
    above that shitty yellow house

where food burned most every night
    where mites ate the grain

where a mouse found its way
    into the refrigerator and died

where it wasn't even an allegory
    to say a snake bit my ring finger. It was supposed to be

restorative, refreshing. It was supposed to be
    more wholesome.

A lot of men died that summer
    but it's you I want to tell

that I wish you had done what you wanted to
    back in one of our city's fine high rises

before you forgot yourself and before I
    weighed more than you. I wish you had jumped

from your balcony down
    to that courtyard cliché

and either broke or drowned or emerged

triumphant, glittering like the rainbow
    you pointed out to me at a gas station

in Santa Monica, born from the grease stains
    on the asphalt as you were pulling away.

Deception

I was a cheat in morning, in silk silted with floor dirt,
dust growing dust, sorrow kneeling at my stomp.

There was a way to save me; there was a book on it.
There was one more state. In California, they fill all

ashtrays with fresh sand, all vehicles with the mad.
Dog-woman, knife fight, the man who said he was a man,

who swore to it licking my arm upon exit. It is this nature
that hurt in the sun, despite what love I was in.

I do in yellow ruffle but choose the grotesque for myself,
the runt rodent beating its heart in my hand.

What pool is this? What balcony? I must always
be reconciled. What gift I bought or dance I made.

White chickens and tapestry, fog on the fireworks.

Champion

As a doll I flew on a plane for a lover convinced
his fists uncovering my blood meant *win*. I was wrong

and found in radiant grasses. I was wild-caught, kept
polite in my madness. There was a team

waged to champion that withery girl: one for trapping
my arm with Velcro and band, one to inform

me hourly I had a face and that face bid eyes
and they were green. I walked once down a darkly

orange stairwell, all flickering lamp docile, worn out
but tractable. I am done being tractable.

This is the brave new me and I know: what I would do
if I could undo zippered backs of my own

blue dresses. What I would learn from the listing
of birdcalls. What I would say for deserved

and desire: I would not even break to tell you.

Poem for a Daughter

Here's a dustbowl drenched in eucalyptus
in the middle of nowhere
where I've been some dozen times.
Here's a fire hydrant, brilliant, swallowed
by the shrunken brush. I hug it like it loves me,
lick it like it's mine. I'm itching
and aching and bored. I need you to be born.
Make new what was never new, make it rain.
I'm killing bees with my bare hands.
I've ridden all the stable horses.
When I use a canteen
I love the word canteen.
I have lived on earth for thirty-one years now.

At twelve my legs gave on the bend.
At twenty I held a posy so close I hated it,
panicked, gave it away to ghosts.
Today you are inside me, promising,
swelling us, what kind of miracle
sitting down would be.
On the next hill there's a movie set
or a pep rally, it's hard to tell in the shimmering heat.
It's all tumbledown menacing, maybe a clothesline.
Windbreak branches ornament with intent,
litter the ground with their gum.
We aren't native to this land.
It's time to plant what is. It's time to go home.

Superstar Hollywood Home Tours

It wasn't that bad. Sometimes
it was almost beautiful.

I took grungy day hikes near Mulholland
and got them over with.

I visited ramshackle food huts
and strolled spray-painted back alleys.

I graced the dishonored mansions
of dead legends, gilded mirrors

even in the guest bathrooms.
I went to recovery clinics

and church basements, museum cafes
and the side chapels of synagogues.

I tried on dozens of mediocre hot pants
at the thrift store on Melrose, inhaling the musty

synthetics of someone else's bygone youth.
I was starting to understand history, geography.

I went to the baseball card store.
I went to the penthouse suite.

I went persistently to strangers
and took all the candy they handed me

with a most disarming smile.
I meant to be cleansed way out in the Valley

only to be told my third eye was blinking.
I attended two and a half communist youth meetings.

I rarely knew where I was going
if I wasn't going on a bus line.

I rarely knew where I was going
when I shut the door of whoever's car.

I kissed a young Republican on a small, docked boat.
I day tripped one beach and then another.

I suffered a dangerous amount
of burning flesh, of fertility, of amnesia.

I missed a lot of school.
It wasn't that bad but I think the map

I bought from a friendly man in a fishing hat
outside the laundromat near Fountain and Vine

the one who tried to guess my age
and fix the color of my aura

was a map to the homes of the stars
with enough cartooning to please a child

and enough useless information to please the frenzy
when what I needed was a map to what I had

too long overlooked, the genuine people and ideas,
the staggering landscapes and the sun-struck

flora because sometimes it was so
stupidly beautiful, like the hummingbird

trumpet outside the nursing home on Fairfax
or the lime tree in front of my parents' apartment

that I had never noticed but that had been there
the whole time.

Oh Funny Birdsong Oh Love

The letters I send to others
won't reroute or reply; it is only us.
Please if you would stride
a length to me; I will not forget
not to wreck my hands.

This next correspondence
a curtsy to you. Precise. Freaked
with devotion, it will be all there is.
I keep forgetting to tell you.
I saw the flowers spite-grown

ordered outside that moribund house.
They weren't a bit delicate
but spire-stalked and steady.
May this be what happens in place
of grandness: an anyway silk

and altered purple. By chance I fear
everyone but you. By choice
we are the only living thing.
Two pigeons on an inside sill.
Ours will be an unusual bliss.

Niagara

It wasn't God
with us that October.

It was something bigger than we can put into solemn books
and pray to

although I saw you praying as you stood over the falls,

your eyes shut for a while. I was praying too
which I do when I've lost sight

of anything human.
I'll admit it here:

I was embarrassed

because the scene didn't take my breath away like I had wanted it to.
Majestic, yes, and

sure, I could imagine falling
because I always imagine falling

but there was something about the way
the lavender of the sweater you bought me

split open

the mist and the gray
that had me thinking

things don't have to be sweeping to be beautiful,

they don't have to kill me
to make me love them.

Wallflower

It used to be that I was the prize
for stalking shadows, for keeping your trap shut.
I'd paint a corner to set myself in,

round that corner, smash a corner to see
what sprung up next. When I knew you loved me
you let me stay the night.

If I were you I'd erect a staircase and I'd climb
stone by stone just to escape myself.
Believe me, I've tried.

But you wanted me with you.
And I get it now.
The fronds are grooving on their flamingo stalks.

They're all we like about what we call California.
Here's our world, then, a dawn in the distance.
If you had told me, when I could speak only in whispers,

that the light hitting the sickly coral of the beach hotels
could travel further inland
and all the way east to find me,

this spot of a girl, grayer and gray and pink,
I might have hastened from my ambush
angling upward to the moon,

black and gravitational,
upending the illuminated trappings
we cannot live in this life without.

ACKNOWLEDGMENTS

Many thanks go out to the editors of *Isn't It Romantic: 100 Love Poems by Younger American Poets* (Verse) and to the editors of the following journals in which some of these poems first appeared: *Antioch Review, The Awl, Bomb, Boston Review, The Brooklyn Rail, The Cortland Review, Denver Quarterly, Gallerie (India), Guernica, Gulf Coast, Jerry, The Journal, jubilat, LIT, Maggy, Narrative, The Paris Review, Poetry Daily, A Public Space, This Land Press.* Thanks also to Anticipated Stranger for publishing some of these poems in the limited-edition chapbook *Six Poems*.

Passionate gratitude to my friends and family for their years of love and support. Thanks to my teachers, especially David Swanger, Richard Howard, and Lucie Brock-Broido. And to the late Phil Bosakowski, who first gave me hope. For their advice, their brilliance, and their wild faith in me and my poems, thanks to Timothy Donnelly, Brett Fletcher Lauer, Mark Bibbins, Mary Jo Bang, Rachel Boynton, and Steven Shainberg.

Thanks to KMA Sullivan, for getting me so completely, and to Justin Boening, for bringing us together.

A lifetime of thanks to Anita and Michael Melnick, for all the love and all the books.

And to Ada and Stella Donnelly, who give me all the hope I'll ever need.

NOTES

"There Was a Child Who Never Wanted," "Dance You Monster to My Soft Song!," "A Genie Serves a Continental Breakfast, Angel Brings the Desired," and "Wallflower" all take their titles from, and are written after, work by Paul Klee.

"The Rain is Over, Apparently" takes its title from A.C. Baldwin's 1853 book *The Traveler's Vade Mecum; or Instantaneous Letter Writer, by Mail or Telegraph, for the Convenience of Persons Traveling on Business or for Pleasure, and for Others, Whereby a Vast Amount of Time, Labor, and Trouble is Saved.*

The italicized words in "Monstrous" are from Emily Brontë's untitled poem beginning "I'll come when thou art saddest."

The title for "And If Thou Wilt, Forget" comes from Christina Rosetti's "Song."

"Diorama" was written after the sculpture "Diorama, 1982" by Thomas Hirschhorn. Much thanks to Ada Donnelly for her help with this poem.

Some of the phrases in "When California Arrives It Lasts All Year" are taken from the folk song "My Darling Clementine."

"A Description Is Not a Birthday" takes its title from Gertrude Stein's *Tender Buttons.*

"If I Should Say I Have Hope" takes its title and some phrasing from the Bible's Book of Ruth.

Also from YesYes Books

Full-length Collections

Heavy Petting by Gregory Sherl

Panic Attack, USA by Nate Slawson

I Don't Mind If You're Feeling Alone
by Thomas Patrick Levy

The Youngest Butcher in Illinois by Robert Ostrom

Vinyl 45s
a limited run print chapbook series

Please Don't Leave Me Scarlett Johansson
by Thomas Patrick Levy

Pepper Girl by Jonterri Gadson

Poetry Shots
a digital chapbook series

Nocturne Trio
with poetry by Metta Sáma and art by Mihret Dawit

Toward What Is Awful
with poetry by Dana Guthrie Martin and art by Ghangbin Kim

How to Survive a Hotel Fire
with poetry by Angela Veronica Wong and art by Megan Laurel

The Blue Teratorn
with poetry by Dorothea Lasky and art by Kaori Mitsushima

My Hologram Chamber Is Surrounded by Miles of Snow
with poetry by Ben Mirov and images by Eric Amling